American History Arts & Crafts

LEARNING ABOUT THE
CIVIL RIGHTS MOVEMENT
WITH ARTS & CRAFTS

Kira Freed

PowerKiDS press

New York

Published in 2015 by **The Rosen Publishing Group, Inc.**
29 East 21st Street, New York, NY 10010

Library of Congress Cataloging-in-Publication-Data

Freed, Kira.
 Learning about the civil rights movement with arts & crafts / Kira Freed.
   pages cm. — (American history arts & crafts)
 Includes index.
ISBN 978-1-4777-5860-1 (pbk.)
ISBN 978-1-4777-5862-5 (6 pack)
ISBN 978-1-4777-5857-1 (library binding)
1. African Americans—Civil rights—History—20th century—Juvenile literature. 2. African
Americans—Civil rights—History—Study and teaching—Activity programs—Juvenile literature.
I. Title. II. Title: Learning about the civil rights movement with arts and crafts.
 E185.61.F8396 2015
 323.1196'0730904—dc23
                        2014033927

Developed and produced for Rosen by BlueAppleWorks Inc.
Art Director: T. J. Choleva
Managing Editor for BlueAppleWorks: Melissa McClellan
Photo Research: Jane Reid
Editor: Marcia Abramson
Craft Consultant: Jerrie McClellan

Photo Credits:
Cover USIA/Public Domain; title page, p. 10–11, 19, 24–25, 28–29 Austen Photography; p. 4 top Library of Congress/
Public Domain; p. 4–5 bottom/Public Domain; p. 5 left Alfred Waud/Public Domain; p. 6 bottom John Vachon for U.S.
Farm Security Administration/Public Domain; p.6 top and left, 22 Jack Delano/Library of Congress/Public Domain; p. 7
right Library of Congress/Public Domain; p. 7 left John T. Bledsoe/Library of Congress/Public Domain; p.8–9 bottom, 16,
18 left Marion S. Trikosko/Library of Congress/Public Domain; p. 8 top John Collier/Library of Congress/Public Domain;
p. 8 left Al. Ravenna/Library of Congress/Public Domain; p. 9 right DOJ photographer/Public Domain; cover top right,
p. 10 left Gvictoria/Dreamstime; p. 12 top Pete Souza/Public Domain; p. 12 left USIA/Public Domain; p. 12–13 bottom,
16–17 bottom Thomas J. O'Halloran/Public Domain; p. 13 right © Jack Moebes/Corbis; p. 14 left Dick DeMarsico/
Library of Congress/Public Domain; p. 14 bottom, 20–21 bottom Warren K. Leffler/Library of Congress/Public Domain;
p. 16 top Library of Congress/Public Domain; p. 17 Carol Highsmith/Library of Congress/Public Domain; p. 18 right
Studiobarcelona/Brad Calkins/Batman2000/Dreamstime; p. 20 top National Park Service/Public Domain; p. 21 top
Department of Defense/Public Domain; p. 21 bottom Public Domain; p. 22 top Thomas Kelly/Library of Congress/Public
Domain; p. 23 bottom Peter Pettus/Library of Congress/Public Domain; p. 23 right Yoichi R. Okamoto/Public Domain;
cover middle right, p. 24 left maxstockphoto/Shutterstock; p. 24 middle Aleksandr Ugorenkov/Dreamstime; p. 26 top ©
James L. Amos/Corbis; p. 26 United States Information Agency/Public Domain; p. 27 top spirit of america/Shutterstock;
p. 27 bottom left Somartin/Dreamstime; cover bottom right, p. 27 bottom right Rena Schild/Shutterstock; p. 28 left
Adam Zivner/Creative Commons; p. 28 bottom right Aigarsr/Dreamstime

Manufactured in the United States of America
CPSIA Compliance Information: Batch #CW15PK For Further Information contact: Rosen Publishing, New York, New York at 1-800-237-9932

Table of Contents

Slavery in America

In 1619, a Dutch ship carrying African slaves docked near the Virginia colony of Jamestown. The slaves, who were brought in chains, had been captured as labor for the colony's tobacco crop. Historians point to that landing as the beginning of slavery in what is now the United States. The practice of slavery would last for close to 250 years before being **abolished**.

Around 20 African captives arrived in late August 1619 aboard a Dutch warship. They were sold and traded into servitude for supplies.

Slaves were considered property rather than human beings and were often treated with **brutality**. They were considered **inferior** to whites and were kept completely dependent upon slave owners.

DID YOU KNOW?

In 1807, the United States passed a law abolishing the African slave trade. The law stopped slaves from being brought to the United States from other countries. However, the South already had more than four million slaves, and American citizens were still allowed to buy and sell slaves within United States borders.

Slavery Gradually Ends

After the United States was founded in 1776, the northern states gradually abolished slavery, but slavery continued in the South. Plantation owners used slaves for agricultural work, which was especially hard during the South's intense summers. Slaves in cities worked as common laborers as well as in skilled trades. Some slaves tried to escape, either to the North or to Canada.

In the early 1860s, the North and South battled each other during the Civil War. Slavery was outlawed at the end of the Civil War.

Plantation owners used slaves mostly to work in their vast fields. Some slaves worked as domestic servants.

Three amendments to the U.S. Constitution became law soon after the Civil War ended in 1865. The Thirteenth Amendment (1865) abolished slavery. The Fourteenth Amendment (1868) established that all people born or naturalized in the United States, regardless of race, were citizens. This amendment also forbade states from limiting the basic rights of citizens. The Fifteenth Amendment (1870) granted all men the right to vote, regardless of race, color, or "previous condition of servitude" (enslavement).

African Americans were granted the right to vote 251 years after the first African captives arrived in Jamestown.

Segregation

Although African Americans were no longer slaves and had gained protection from three new Constitutional amendments, their freedom to enjoy the same rights as other U.S. citizens was still sharply **restricted**. African Americans outnumbered whites in many places in the South. Many white people feared the possibility of former slaves working together and gaining political power. As a result, white Southerners prevented African Americans from gaining equality or political and economic power.

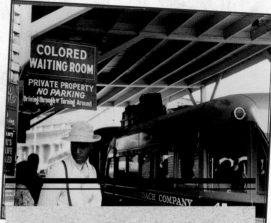

Bus stations in the South had separate waiting areas for African American and white people.

African Americans were allowed to drink only from public fountains marked "Colored." Colored was an early word for African Americans.

Restaurants as well had separate sections for African American and white customers.

Jim Crow Laws

A series of **segregation** laws, known as Jim Crow laws, were passed, mainly in the South and in border states. Although these laws were presented as granting African Americans "separate but equal" status, in truth the laws were crafted to restrict civil rights. African Americans had to use separate drinking fountains and restrooms. Segregation was the law in housing, jobs, public schools, transportation, and public places, including restaurants and parks. African Americans had poorer jobs, homes, schools, and hospitals.

WHO WAS JIM CROW?

Jim Crow laws were named for a character in a song. Thomas Dartmouth Rice, a struggling white actor, heard a black person singing "Jump Jim Crow" and started using it in his own routine in 1828. Rice dressed as a foolish black character who sang, danced, and grinned. He was one of the first to perform in blackface makeup, darkening his skin with burned cork. His performances led "Jim Crow" to become an insulting term for an African American.

Early sheet music for the song "Jump Jim Crow" shows a caricature of African Americans. The phrase "Jim Crow" comes from the song.

Supporters of Jim Crow laws defended segregation by claiming that white people were better than African Americans.

The Civil Rights Movement Begins

Challenges to the injustice of the Jim Crow system began early on. The National Association for the Advancement of Colored People (NAACP) was founded in 1910. The NAACP called for full political equality for African Americans and an end to racial **discrimination**. This organization continues to be a strong voice for **justice** and equality today.

The founders of the civil rights movement had the future of young African Americans in mind when they began working together to bring segregation laws to an end.

In another early effort, African American railroad workers demanded higher wages and better working conditions. The Brotherhood of Sleeping Car Porters used **strikes**, marches, **demonstrations**, and court battles to advance their cause successfully.

NAACP leaders and Thurgood Marshall (right) worked together to help end racial discrimination.

A Stunning Victory

The tide turned with a 1954 court case. The NAACP sued the Board of Education in Topeka, Kansas, for preventing an African American girl from attending an all-white public school. A brilliant lawyer named Thurgood Marshall argued *Brown v. Board of Education* before the U.S. Supreme Court. Marshall proved that African American and white schools did not receive equal amounts of money and of teachers. He also proved that segregation caused African American children to feel bad about themselves and damaged their ability to learn. The Supreme Court outlawed segregated schools in 1954. However, it would take more work to make **integration** a reality.

RUBY BRIDGES

Many whites opposed the Supreme Court ruling, and Southern schools were slow to integrate. Finally a federal court ordered schools to desegregate. Ruby Bridges, a six-year-old African American girl, was chosen to attend an all-white school in New Orleans, Louisiana. For an entire year, she was the only African American student at the school. Many white parents kept their children at home. Ruby faced an angry mob on her way into the school every day, but government officers protected her. The next year, African American and white students attended the school together.

U.S. marshals escorted Ruby Bridges to and from school to protect her from angry mobs.

Craft to Make:

Tambourine

Music played a key role in the civil rights movement. It was sung on marches, at meetings, in jails, and at performance halls. The song "We Shall Overcome," the movement's unofficial anthem, gave people courage and hope amid the struggles. Folk, gospel, and blues were three major threads of civil rights music. Instruments such as guitars and tambourines accompanied voices.

Freedom songs inspired people and stirred them to action.

What You Will Need

- Large empty box (thin cardboard)
- 8 inch (20 cm) wide bowl
- Pen and ruler
- Scissors
- Glue
- Masking and duct tape
- Paint and brush
- 6 small bells
- Ribbon

Step One

Unfold your box and lay it out flat. Measure an 8½ inch (22 cm) square. Cut the corners off. Put your bowl on the cardboard and trace around it with your pen. Add marks all around your circle about ½ inch (1.3 cm) long. Cut all the small marks to the inner circle.

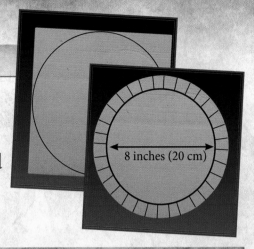

8 inches (20 cm)

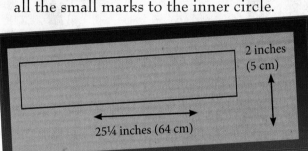

2 inches (5 cm)

25¼ inches (64 cm)

Step Two

Draw a rectangle on the cardboard to the sizes shown. Cut it out.

Step Three

Press the tabs of the circle up and put glue on the back of each one. Press the rectangle against the tabs. Tape the tabs to the rectangle piece with duct tape.

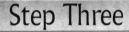

Step Four

Cover the entire tambourine with masking tape to make it stronger. Paint the outside of the tambourine.

Step Five

Make 6 holes in the side of the tambourine using the tip of your scissors. Cut 12 long pieces of ribbon. Pull 2 pieces of ribbon through the bell and tie a knot leaving enough ribbon at one end to pull through the hole in the tambourine. Pull the ends of the ribbon through a hole, tie a knot, and tape over the knot and leftover ribbon with duct tape. Repeat with the other bells. Decorate your tambourine. Make some noise!

Rosa Parks

A seamstress named Rosa Parks is considered the mother of the civil rights movement. Parks lived in Montgomery, Alabama. On December 1, 1955, while returning home by bus from a long day of work, Parks sat down in a seat in the middle of the bus. Montgomery law required African

In 2012, President Barack Obama visited the Henry Ford Museum in Michigan where the famous Rosa Parks bus is displayed. Parks was arrested sitting in the same row Obama is in, but on the opposite side.

Americans to give up a middle seat if a white person wanted it. When the bus driver ordered Parks to give up her seat, she refused. She didn't argue or become angry—she just stayed in her seat. After the bus driver called the police, Parks was arrested. When Rosa Parks refused to give up her bus seat, she knew she would be arrested. As an active member of the NAACP, she wanted to take a stand against segregation.

Rosa Parks (1913-2005) is considered the mother of the civil rights movement.

The Montgomery Bus Boycott

African American leaders in Montgomery called for a bus **boycott** on December 5, 1955, the day of Parks's trial. They asked African Americans to stay off buses to **protest** the arrest and trial. African Americans walked, shared rides, took taxis, or rode bicycles or even mules, but they didn't ride the buses.

The bus boycott lasted for over a year and cost the city of Montgomery a huge amount of money. Just over a year after Rosa Parks refused to give up her seat, the U.S. Supreme Court ruled that segregated transportation was **unconstitutional**.

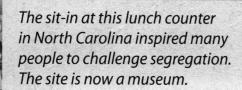

The sit-in at this lunch counter in North Carolina inspired many people to challenge segregation. The site is now a museum.

Martin Luther King Jr.

A local minister named Dr. Martin Luther King Jr. was the head of the organization that led the bus boycott. Dr. King was a strong believer in the power of **nonviolent resistance**. He urged people to meet hatred with love and be willing to be arrested and jailed rather than fight back.

The success of the bus boycott showed the world that nonviolent protest could bring about change. In 1957, Dr. King and other leaders founded the Southern Christian Leadership Conference (SCLC) to find other opportunities to practice nonviolent resistance to segregation.

Dr. King attracted thousands of supporters from all backgrounds with his beliefs.

Dr. Martin Luther King Jr. (1929-1968) still inspires people all over the world to work peacefully for justice.

The Birmingham Campaign

In 1963, Birmingham, Alabama, became a focus of the SCLC's efforts to end segregation. Known for its violence and racism, Birmingham was one of the most segregated cities in the country. A boycott was called with the goal of pressuring business leaders to create more jobs for African Americans and end segregation in stores and restaurants. When business leaders failed to cooperate, the SCLC organized marches and sit-ins meant to result in the arrests of many protesters. Dr. King and other SCLC leaders believed that filling the jails would force city leaders to listen.

The SCLC was the main organizing power that led nonviolent protests in support of civil rights reform. Dr. King led the SCLC until his death.

The Children's March

African Americans in Birmingham wanted segregation to end, but they were afraid that getting involved would lead to violence or the loss of their jobs. One of the SCLC leaders thought

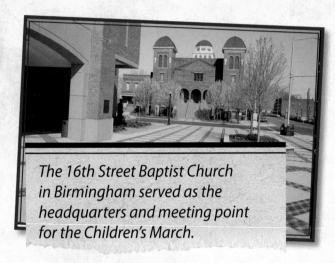

The 16th Street Baptist Church in Birmingham served as the headquarters and meeting point for the Children's March.

of involving students in the protests. He taught them about civil rights and showed them a movie in which nonviolent protesters were attacked. As a result, many students became active in the effort to end segregation.

SCLC leaders planned a peaceful children's protest march in Birmingham on May 2, 1963. The police chief said the children had no permit to march. When the march began, over one thousand children were arrested.

Hundreds of students left their schools in order to be arrested, set free, and then to get arrested again the next day.

Police Violence

The jails were almost full on the second day of the march. Birmingham's police chief ordered the use of fire hoses and attack dogs to stop the protest. Radio and television around the world carried news of the police brutality.

Civil rights leaders and protesters refused to stop the protests. President John F. Kennedy sent government representatives to Birmingham to force city officials to **negotiate** with civil rights leaders. An agreement resulted in the integration of Birmingham's public facilities. African Americans were allowed to work in stores, and protesters were released from jail.

This sculpture honors the civil rights marchers of Birmingham, Alabama. It is in Ingram Park, where many were arrested.

THIS SCULPTURE IS DEDICATED TO THE FOOT SOLDIERS OF THE BIRMINGHAM CIVIL RIGHTS MOVEMENT.

WITH GALLANTRY, COURAGE AND GREAT BRAVERY THEY FACED THE VIOLENCE OF ATTACK DOGS, HIGH POWERED WATER HOSES, AND BOMBINGS. THEY WERE THE FODDER IN THE ADVANCE AGAINST INJUSTICE, WARRIORS OF A JUST CAUSE; THEY REPRESENT HUMANITY UNSHAKEN IN THEIR FIRM BELIEF IN THEIR NATION'S COMMITMENT TO LIBERTY AND JUSTICE FOR ALL.

WE SALUTE THESE MEN AND WOMEN WHO WERE THE SOLDIERS OF THIS GREAT CAUSE.

RICHARD ARRINGTON
MAYOR OF BIRMINGHAM
MAY 1995

17

Craft to Make:

Civil Rights Poster

Many young people learned about the date of the Children's March through flyers asking them to gather at Birmingham's Sixteenth Street Baptist Church on May 2, 1963. Flyers helped spread the word about protest marches throughout the civil rights movement. Protesters often carried signs and banners, either printed or hand drawn, during demonstrations.

the **Time** is always right to **DO** the **right THING**

Martin Luther King Jr.

Typical banners carried phrases such as "We march for integrated schools," "Protest injustice," "Separate is not equal," and "Equal rights for ALL!"

What You Will Need

- Paper or cardboard
- Colored pencils, markers, pastels, or paints
- Glue (optional)

Step One

Words can be very powerful. Create a poster using nothing but text. Search on the computer for a short quote from Martin Luther King Jr. that inspires you. Sketch out some of your ideas and see what works best.

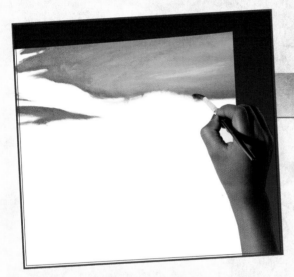

Step Two

Create a background; it can be all one color or a blend of colors. Try using different techniques and mediums. Paint the poster first and then make streaks with pastels. Have fun.

Step Three

There are two ways to create the type. One is to write the words yourself directly on the poster. The other is to use a computer and printer. Write your quote in a word program, and then print the words out and glue them to the poster. Make some of the words bigger than others to emphasize them. Make some of the words different colors.

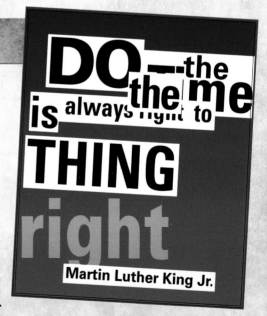

The Civil Rights Address

One month after the Children's March, President Kennedy gave a speech called the Civil Rights Address. Kennedy called civil rights a moral issue, meaning that it involved knowing the difference between right and wrong. He said that although slavery had been abolished one hundred years earlier, African Americans were still targets of **injustice**. Kennedy proposed a law that would outlaw discrimination on the basis of race, color, religion, sex, or country of origin. The law would establish equal treatment in workplaces, public schools, and other public facilities. It would also strengthen voting rights.

President Kennedy gave his Civil Rights Address on June 11, 1963, after sending troops to help two African American students enter the University of Alabama. He asked all Americans to end unjust discrimination.

People jammed the National Mall from the Lincoln Memorial to the Washington Monument for the March on Washington in 1963. It remains one of the largest protests ever held in the U.S. capital.

March on Washington

Civil rights leaders organized a huge demonstration on August 28, 1963, in Washington, D.C. More than 200,000 people took part in the March on Washington to show their support for equal rights and the law that President Kennedy had proposed. Marchers gathered in front of the Lincoln Memorial and listened to speeches and songs about equality.

During the March on Washington, Dr. King gave his famous "I Have a Dream" speech about his vision of freedom, justice, and equality for all Americans.

Although President Kennedy was **assassinated** three months later, the law he proposed became the Civil Rights Act of 1964. President Lyndon B. Johnson signed it into law on July 2, 1964.

The signing of the Civil Rights Act of 1964 by President Lyndon B. Johnson was shown on national television.

Voting Rights for All

The Fifteenth Amendment guaranteed African American men the right to vote, and the Civil Rights Act of 1964 required voting rules to be applied equally to all races. Nevertheless, Southern states used various policies to prevent African Americans from voting. For example, election officials often required **literacy** tests. If they wanted the test taker to pass, they asked simple questions such as "Who is the president of the United States?" If officials wanted the test taker to fail, they asked impossibly hard questions, limited the amount of time for the test, or required a perfect score.

This poster created in 1871 shows the celebrations of the signing of the Fifteenth Amendment in 1870.

DID YOU KNOW?

In addition to literacy tests, some states used poll taxes to deny the right to vote. Many African Americans were too poor to pay a tax in order to vote. A "grandfather clause" said that voters did not have to pay a tax or take a test if their grandfather could vote, but this did not help most African Americans. Their grandfathers, as slaves, had not been allowed to vote.

Selma, Alabama

Civil rights leaders worked across the South to register African Americans to vote. To protest the murder of several civil rights workers, leaders planned a march from Selma to Montgomery, Alabama, on March 7, 1965. Before the marchers left Selma, police officers stopped them with violence. People across the country were horrified by the police brutality. They demanded that the voting rights of all U.S. citizens be protected.

President Johnson signed the Voting Rights Act of 1965 in August. The law made it illegal to introduce any voting law used for racial discrimination.

Voting protects people's right to be treated fairly by giving them a voice in their government. They can elect public officials who represent their concerns and who make decisions on their behalf. Being denied the right to vote is an important sign that a group of people also lack other rights and freedoms. President Johnson considered the vote "the most powerful instrument ever devised…for breaking down injustice."

Dr. King joined President Johnson in 1965 for the signing of the Voting Rights Act.

The 1965 Selma to Montgomery march led to the passage of the 1965 Voting Rights Act.

Craft to Make:

Freedom Hands

The civil rights movement did not only involve African Americans, and they weren't the only ones who stood to benefit from it. It was in the interests of all people to work to create a country that guaranteed equal rights for all and valued the contributions of every citizen. People of every race, religion, and cultural background—including large numbers of white people—were active in the civil rights movement. The image of "freedom hands" became a symbol of equality among people of every color and the celebration of human diversity.

What You Will Need

- Craft paper
- Pencil and scissors
- Glue
- Paper or foam plate
- Double-sided tape
- Cardboard or sponge
- Poster board (optional)

Step One

Trace your hand on a piece of paper. Cut out and then use this as a pattern to cut out many hands from different colors of paper. Cut out at least 10 hands.

Step Two

Glue the hands you have cut out around the paper plate.

Step Three

Find images of the world and a dove online and print them. You could also draw them yourself. Cut the world image out and glue it in the center.

Step Four

Cut the dove out. Glue a sponge (or cardboard) to the back, and then glue the sponge to the plate. If you like, use double-sided tape to mount the plate on a poster board, and then decorate.

The Struggle Continues

Dr. King continued to be a leading voice in the civil rights movement after the passage of the Civil Rights Act and Voting Rights Act. In the spring of 1968, at age 39, he went to Memphis, Tennessee, to lead a garbage workers' strike for higher wages and better working conditions. As he stood on a motel balcony, he was killed by an assassin's bullet. An estimated 100,000 people attended Dr. King's funerals and a funeral procession that ended with the singing of "We Shall Overcome."

President Johnson declared a national day of mourning for the lost civil rights leader on April 7, 1968.

Dr. King's nonviolent efforts to achieve equality were honored in 1964, when he was awarded the Nobel Peace Prize.

New generations of people carry on Dr. King's dream by continuing to work for freedom and justice for all Americans.

Remembering Dr. King

In 1983, President Ronald Reagan signed a law creating a national holiday to honor Dr. King's tireless work to end discrimination. The holiday is celebrated in January for Dr. King's birthday. In many areas it is a day of service offering Americans an opportunity to help others.

The civil rights movement has made great strides since the 1960s. However, discrimination has not yet been wiped out, and the movement's mission has not yet been fully achieved.

CIVIL RIGHTS BUTTONS

Buttons were popular among civil rights demonstrators. Marchers often wore buttons with sayings such as "I Have a Dream," "We Shall Overcome," and "Freedom NOW!" Try making your own button:

1. Purchase a kit for making snap-in plastic buttons from a craft store.
2. Create the image for your button, either by hand or on a computer. The kit includes instructions about the size. Carefully cut out your image.
3. Place your image facedown in the bowl-shaped piece from the kit. Place the bottom of the image closest to you.
4. Snap the back into place with the pin horizontal at the top.

Craft to Make:

Peace Beads

Martin Luther King Jr. was dedicated to peaceful approaches to change throughout his life. In his last years, he voiced his objections to the Vietnam War. Many young people in the 1960s, also strongly committed to peace, admired Dr. King. Called "hippies," they decorated themselves and their belongings with symbols of peace. These symbols included a dove and a large flower representing "flower power," a term for power or influence achieved through peaceful means instead of force. Peace symbols often appeared in necklaces made of beads.

The peace sign was another popular symbol that to this day represents a wish for peace.

What You Will Need

- Paper
- Pen and ruler
- Scissors
- Toothpicks
- Clear glue
- Styrofoam cup
- Wire or pipe cleaners
- Thin string

Step One

Gather the paper you want to use; it can be old magazines, junk mail or craft paper. Mark your paper to match the illustration. The triangle should be one inch (2.5 cm) on the bottom and as long as your paper. The length of the paper determines how thick your bead will be. Cut out 22 triangles.

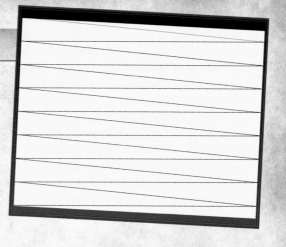

Step Two

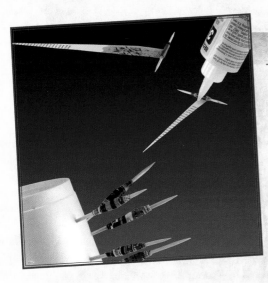

Start with the wide end of the paper and start rolling it on the toothpick. Roll it as tight as you can. When you get near the end, apply glue to the inside of the paper. Continue to roll the paper to the end. Press down for a few seconds to make sure the glue holds. Stick the toothpick into a Styrofoam cup to let it dry. Repeat until you have made all 22 beads.

Step Three

Cut a piece of string more than twice as long as you want your necklace to be. Tie a knot leaving about 3 inches (8 cm) extra. Slide the first bead through to that knot. Tie a knot and then put the next bead on. Continue until you are almost out of string and then tie a double knot.

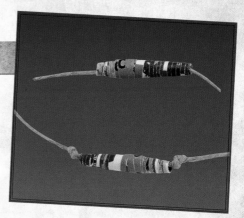

Step Four

Make a peace sign by twisting either wire or pipe cleaners as shown in the photo. Use the middle piece to attach it to the necklace.

Glossary

abolished Put an end to; outlawed.

assassinated Murdered (especially an important person) by a surprise attack.

boycott A form of protest in which people refuse to take part in something in order to force a change.

brutality Extreme violence or cruelty.

demonstrations Events in which people gather to express their support of or opposition to a cause.

discrimination The unfair treatment of a person or group based on race, sex, religion, age, or other differences.

inferior Of less value or importance.

injustice Unfair treatment that includes limitations on rights and freedoms.

integration The end of a policy that forces people of different races to stay separate in a certain location.

justice The act of being fair and honest.

literacy The state or quality of being able to read and write.

negotiate To have a discussion for the purpose of reaching an agreement.

nonviolent resistance The practice of using peaceful means to achieve political goals.

protest An event organized for the purpose of expressing strong disagreement or disapproval.

racism The belief that one race is better than another; poor treatment of, or violence against, people based on such a belief.

restricted Limited or controlled.

segregation A policy that forces people of different races to stay separate in a certain location.

strikes Protests in which people stop working in order to force a change in working conditions.

unconstitutional Not following the United States Constitution.

For More Information

Further Reading

Adamson, Heather. *The Civil Rights Movement: An Interactive History of America.* Capstone Press, 2009.

McDonough, Yona Zeldis. *Who Was Rosa Parks?*
Grosset & Dunlap, 2010.

McWhorter, Diane. *A Dream of Freedom.* Scholastic, 2004.

Websites

Due to the changing nature of Internet links, PowerKids Press has developed an online list of websites related to the subject of this book. This site is updated regularly. Please use this link to access the list:
www.powerkidslinks.com/ahac/crm

Index